The Adaptive St

CW01052195

Other Hollin Books:

Power Coaching
The Too Busy Trap
The Steps Before Step One
Notes on Behavioural Management Techniques
Ideas For Wimps
How To Escape From Cloud Cuckoo Land
How To Empty The Too Hard Box
Safety Leadership
BMT Scorecards

Many thanks to everyone who read the drafts, fed back, contributed to and influenced this book; Dr Richard Kazbour, Bruce Faulkner, Craig Reade, Simon Roberts, Aaron Sorkin, Martin Laycock, Iain Humphreys, Garry Sanderson, Dr Nicole Gravina and Dr Denis O'Hora. Special thanks to Jack Sheehan for the advice and the back-cover statement, Alasdair Cathcart for encouragement and the foreword, and Jean Lees for the beautiful front cover photo. Extra special thanks to the Hollin team: Joanne, Rachel, Nicola, Alison, Alan, Claire and Dave. This book was expertly edited by Lynn Dunlop.

Hollin Ltd
Westminster House
10 Westminster Road
Macclesfield
Cheshire
SK10 1BX
howard@hollin.co.uk

First published by Hollin Ltd. January 2019
© Copyright 2019 Hollin Ltd.
Graphics by Creative Hero
ISBN number 978-0-9575211-6-2

Foreword by Alasdair Cathcart

"What?" you may be asking yourself as you pick up this book. Maybe you are someone who is interested in what strategy is, or maybe you have this book because you simply have a passion for learning. Whatever your reason, you probably hope that it will help grow your knowledge, maybe challenge you to consider trying new approaches, and perhaps support you in finding success in today's competitive and evolving business climate. The ideas in this book are simple, the reflections are honest, the examples are relevant and all are communicated clearly. If you are looking for a scientific analysis of strategy, then this book is not for you. Don't worry; you will be given the references that permit further study should you wish; however, I suspect this book will provide everything you will need on the topic.

So what? Well, many businesses or projects operate without a clear strategy. Howard helps us to understand our and our colleagues' frames of reference in order to create an environment that will support a strategy. He challenges us to make tough decisions on what we are and are not going to do in the process. He asks us to keep things simple, balanced even, to support effective communication. He emphasizes that leading and trailing measures are equally important to ensure we deliver to our strategy, while giving us the leeway to adapt.

Howard inspires us to do better by providing examples of attributes that great leaders exhibit in the development and delivery of their strategy. Staying strategic is hard and it requires focus. People need to stay in their ideal zone of involvement, and leaders need to maintain the separation of the consumers and the producers. As someone who mirrored, at various times in his career, at least two of the stereotypical bad leaders that Howard identifies, it is reassuring to note that leadership and strategy development can be learned! His feedback has been instrumental in my leadership development over the twenty years I have known him.

Howard is unique, just like our strategies should be. If you left a copy of your business strategy on the bus, and your competition got on at the next stop and picked it up, would they be able to understand it, but unable to replicate it? That's the true test of an adaptive strategy.

Now what? Read and enjoy this excellent book.

Alasdair Cathcart
President, Bechtel Oil, Gas & Chemicals
Houston, December 2018.

Contents

Section A: Background
1.0 Introduction

Every business or undertaking needs a 'mission', something simple that describes its overall reason for being. The mission of a nurse may be to 'heal the sick'. The mission of a teacher may be to 'create an environment for learning'. In terms of a business or organisation, it may define the product or service to be delivered, perhaps include a customer type and even location. The mission will be something that paints a clear picture of the overall pursuit in fewer than ten words; something that everyone will understand without further explanation.

"Ship this cargo from Liverpool to New York" would be the mission. The choice of vessel, route etc. would be the purview of the manager in charge, and this would be what I would call the strategy. The Captain will set out with a plan and as weather or other circumstances impact the journey, ongoing changes will be made to that strategy in order to satisfy the overall mission and a successful landing in New York. This type of strategy is an Adaptive Strategy.

The mission is fixed, but the strategy is adaptive. This is the basic tenet of this book.

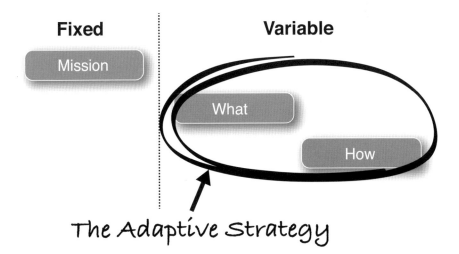

There are interesting discussions to be had when looking back on businesses or projects with problems: Performance issues, compliance issues, 'on time' delivery issues, client relations problems. When I ask questions like "When you started, why did you decide to…", I often get the answer, "We didn't; we didn't decide anything specifically." It turns out that lots of projects and businesses operate with no strategy at all.

A simple strategy like: "This is what we want to do, this is how we will achieve it, and this is how we will know what's really happening along the way" could have helped many cases dramatically. Also, more care with hiring - making sure the right people are in the right seats on the bus before it moves off.

Areas which frequently benefit from a strategic approach include:
- Communication: More consideration regarding how and when to meet, and how to communicate.
- Creating the conditions for success: More consideration as to how a great workplace environment will be created.
- Leadership: More high-level concise statements on the 'what' and the 'how'; simple and respectful messages that everyone will understand and most of them will want to follow.
- Measurement: More clarity as to how everyone will know if it's successful.

This book will not give you an explicit step-by-step solution to all your strategic problems. Your problems are personal, situational and environmental. It will, however, offer a simple framework for you to try out, one that is adaptable to many situations. You must experiment and review, something I cannot do on your behalf.

The book is called The Adaptive Strategy because once the bus moves off, the mission stays the same but everything else is subject to inevitable change over time. Leaders must be making decisions based on the latest information. If the information says, 'change the strategy', then it must be adapted.

1.1 What type of strategy are we talking about?

There are numerous potential strategies and numerous reasons to have strategies; it's a big subject in a very big field. The strategy gurus and consultancies mostly deal with traditional capitalist business scenarios: I have an idea, I borrow some money, hire people, build facilities, sell to clients, expand the business, sell shares, appoint a board of directors etc.

In contrast to this view, I am going to deal with strategy from a behavioural perspective - that is, rather than assuming the strategy takes place in an imaginary aspirational workplace, I will examine the behavioural reasons that strategies succeed or fail. Understanding why people act in the way they do increases the likelihood that your strategy will be designed for today's reality rather than imaginary laboratory conditions.

In this book, I will mention all the scenarios below and some more along the way;
- Personal strategy
- Relationship strategy
- Team strategy
- Business strategy
- Project delivery strategy
- Corporate strategies e.g. growth, stability and renewal

1.2 Research on strategy

I have been immersed in reading and researching strategy this last year. There is a lot of dry stuff out there, lots of comprehensive and detailed business research, strategy information and advice. There's lots of 'strategy in utopia' type advice. Finding really interesting books to read on strategy has been difficult. Some of the luminaries out there worth a scan on the internet include: Dr Max McKeown, Dr Donald Sull, Stephanie Mead, Steven Stowell, Professor Freek Vermeulen, Geoff Donaker and Michael Luca, Margaret Wheatley and Dr Michael E Porter.

Here are some comments from a selection of strategy gurus I researched for this book. I have quoted from what I think were the better books and articles that I read. If you have spare time for internet surfing, then there's a lifetime of information out there on this subject for sure.

Dr Max McKeown said about strategy - 'strategy is shaping the future', 'strategy first, planning second', 'strategy is attaining desirable ends with the available means' and 'strategy is double loop learning'. Dr McKeown's book *The Strategy Book* was the most accessible book I read, as well as the most amusing.

Geoff Donaker and Michael Luca spoke about metrics, and said, 'if you leave chocolate bars in the kitchen, people will eat them', 'if you focus on one metric, expect it to rise at the expense of the other ones' and 'left unchecked, subconscious biases will undermine strategic decision making'.

Margaret Wheatley said that 'leadership is a series of behaviours rather than a role for heroes', 'we don't need more command and control; we need better means to engage everyone's intelligence in solving challenges and crises as they arise', 'everyone in a complex system has a slightly different interpretation. The more interpretations we gather, the easier it becomes to gain a sense of the whole' and 'successful organizations, including the Military, have learned that the higher the risk, the more necessary it is to engage everyone's commitment and intelligence'.

Stephanie S. Mead and Steven Stowell said - 'strategic leaders must not get consumed by the operational and tactical side of their work. They have a duty to find time to shape the future', 'the promise of a better future is what gets team members engaged and unleashes their motivation. When people are invited to be a part of creating the future and can clearly see how they fit in and why they matter, it causes them to do their best work' and 'without the guidance of an insightful leader who can drive the process, it is difficult to make any strategy a reality. Ultimately, strategic leadership is what makes the difference between success and failure'.

Professor Freek Vermeulen said - 'many strategy execution processes fail because the firm does not have something worth executing', 'many so-called strategies are in fact goals', 'spend time on explaining the logic behind your choices' and 'habits in organizations are notoriously sticky and persistent'.

Dr Donald Sull said - 'for a strategy to influence action it must be remembered', 'any strategy that is too complicated to be understood is not a strategy', 'value = costs vs what a customer is willing to pay for it', 'strategy = increasing customers' willingness to pay more OR decreasing the cost of services and goods', and 'there are a small number of key drivers of value creation'. There is a video of Dr Sull on YouTube explaining costs (his left hand) and what customers will pay (his right hand). He says, "My left hand can only go so far down, however the height my right hand can go is limitless!"

Dr Michael Porter said, 'you need a unique value proposition', 'clear trade-offs, including choosing what not to do', 'activities that fit together and reinforce each other' and 'strategic continuity with continual improvement in realising your strategy'. Dr Porter's books are comprehensive; I would say he is the guru's guru. I have been mostly influenced by his work in this project.

1.3 What is being said about strategy

As I reviewed my research, it felt right to summarise broadly what I had read about strategies. Most of the items below are paraphrases, often compilations from a large number of opinions I collected and stuck together in various categories. That's why they're not individually accredited. In short, this is what most of the experts are mostly saying about strategy.

Communication
- Can your strategy accurately be depicted in some simple graphics? Is it one page?
- It's not enough just telling people what you want, always explain why you want it too.
- The launch of a new strategy must show that there are going to be more winners than losers in the business.

- Not explaining the 'win state' for a new strategy can condemn it to failure.
- What are all your unique selling points (USPs)? Do all your people know all your USPs? What other USPs are within reach right now?

Feedback and reporting

- Use data, and beware of sycophants and optimists. They rationalise out the need for accurate feedback, and the worse things get, the more denial ensues.
- Key information must flow up and down unmolested.
- What are the one or two pivotal things you should measure? What are the simple litmus tests that can quickly predict what's going to happen?
- Key information must not be camouflaged by voluminous levels of unnecessary reporting demands. They can create 2nd, 3rd and 4th levels of unwanted camouflage.
- If a business wants to make data-based decisions, then the data must be accurate.
- If your intention is to hit the ball, you must be looking at it.

Marketplace

- It's wise to position your company where the competition forces are the weakest.
- Don't compete in overcrowded or saturated markets.
- Never try to benchmark against your competition; instead focus on describing why you are better.
- If you build intelligence on your client's thinking, then you can then adapt what you do to exploit your client's ever-changing desires/results/KPI's.
- Always be flexible enough to reshape yourself to suit the available work booked.

Customers

- If you build intelligence on your client's thinking, you can then adapt what you do to exploit your client's ever-changing desires/results/KPI's.
- Stop trying to sell stuff no-one wants (anymore).

- Your value proposition to a client must be simple, saleable and easily understood so they will buy from you.
- Make sure you know who owns all your business decisions. If no-one does, then you are screwed. If only the CEO knows, then you are still screwed.
- Your strategy needs to address the question of 'why would your clients want it'?

Common problems

- Most people don't do strategy. Those that try just write a shopping list of desirable results instead.
- Organisations change (perceived) strategy often. Many of them change strategy when the real problem is an inability to execute effectively.

1.4 Strategy in a nutshell

> *"If you don't know where you are going, any road will get you there."* - **Lewis Carroll**

Our innate abilities as humans include the competences to think and plan. I cannot stress enough the importance of having a strategy for any venture. Prior to embarking on writing your strategy there are a number of basics that need defining. To understand the full challenge, it's paramount that you know what's truly happening now. This may necessitate an accurate survey, assessment and analysis so that all voided assumptions (wishful thinking) can be discounted. Most of the experts also agree that you must decide what you are prepared to do and what you are not prepared to do.

Perhaps then write a set of simple results you would like to achieve. Have a think about the interactions and relationships between the people involved in delivering this strategy. Then design a functional feedback loop that tells you what is actually happening as the strategy is executed. Review the strategy monthly, perhaps quarterly, and adapt it.

I have summarised it here:
1. Observe what's happening now
2. Write a simple plan for change (What? Who? Where? When? Why? How?)
3. Roll out and test the plan
4. Gather feedback, analyse and adapt the plan accordingly
5. Iterate

1.5 The traditional business – basic questions

Every business should find out what's actually happening right now. Ask everyone to answer this simple list of questions;
- What are we doing, where, with whom, for whom, when and why?
- What are our long-term ambitions?
- What should we stop doing?
- What do we have that no-one else has?
- What do we do that no-one else does?
- What are our resources, what else do we need, what/who can go?
- What are our capabilities?
- Can we sustain what we have; what are our key threats over time?
- What are our most productive activities?

This boils down simply to:
What? Who? Where? When? Why? and How?

1.6 The bottom line

Designing a strategy requires time and focus; a winning strategy cannot be improvised, strategy needs focus. Execution of a winning strategy requires a solid chain of accurate feedback. When a strategy fails, key points of failure in the strategy can often be traced back to someone's ego. Strategy unzips at the point it meets someone's ego. Keeping ego out of execution is a very hard-won goal and requires leaders to make hard choices and have accurate planning, excellent feedback loops, super-human strength and the determination to stick to the task.

Strategic thinking can be learned and utilised to help you, your team and your company. It can make your workplace a better and more predictable place to be.

2.0 Frame of Reference

"Shift your frame of reference. Realise that all you see around you, the reality you perceive, is a small stage upon which you act." - **Alex Bennet**

Your frame of reference is the coalescence of what you see now and what you have experienced in the past. A personal frame of reference is a set of assumptions and beliefs that one lives one's life by. This is the basis of a person's day to day verbal behaviour. It can be adjusted when new information arrives (or not). It can be founded in a particular culture or a set of family values. Our frame of reference is our perspective, it's our view of the world.

Someone presenting to a meeting or conference is speaking with the full knowledge of their own frame of reference and probably much less knowledge regarding the frames of reference of the other people in the room. Everyone makes assumptions about other people's frame of reference. Everyone has their own unique, ever-changing frame of reference, it's their view of the world. At work, it's their take on how things will be received in any given workplace environment. Every time new information comes in, people's frames of reference adjust accordingly. Sometimes they get it right and sometimes they get it wrong. Finding out other people's perspectives is a good first step, it will help you communicate better.

The frame of reference for a company can change dramatically very quickly. Every company strategy must bake in something that reflects potential deviations from the plan, and this includes the gap between people's assumptions and reality around what's happening and what's about to happen. If you have a view on what's happening, and your colleagues have a different view, what will you do? What's in place to ensure that optimistic (but unrealistic) aspirations are not guiding the strategy?

From a frame of reference perspective, some people work in dissonant teams every day. Other people work in resonant teams every day, and the rest - all stations in between. In a resonant team, difficult feedback can be discussed without fear. Lots of good stuff gets done in this place. In a dissonant team, people are just looking to avoid threats. Not much good stuff gets done in this place. As an outsider, it is quite easy to detect where teams are on a resonant/dissonant scale just by the general 'mood in the camp'. It can be harder to pin down if you are part of the team, but as a benchmark: If you generally enjoy coming to work, then you're likely part of a resonant team. All high-performing teams will be resonant. Creating a resonant team environment should be a major underpinning of any strategy.

High-performing companies develop a surplus of discretionary effort and they do this via trust. High-performing organisations create resonant teams, and these teams understand the value of reliable communication. I would say that being part of a resonant workplace should be the goal for all knowledge workers - anything else should not be tolerated - but this is less commonplace that you might think. For example, companies that lock down all discretionary spend for their employees may feel comfort that their people are not wasting small sums of money. The other side of this coin is that they should also realise that there's not going to be much trust or discretionary effort out there because of their parsimony.

3.0 What Kills Strategy?

Some leaders think their people follow strategies but in reality, people abide by the reinforcers they experience or perceive in their local environment. Behavioural science says that 'environment drives behaviour' i.e., people 'operate' on the particular local environment they work in. Any strategy that is just a list of results and does not take into account the creation of an environment that will deliver the desired goals will fail. Certainly, not without an inordinate amount of luck, and relying on luck is not a strategy I would recommend.

I guess the most common reason that organisations are ineffective or even fail is that there is no strategy at all. I have visited business and projects in distress and asked what the original plan was. They show me a large signed picture of the senior team at a 'team build' in the early days with a list of laudable aspirations written in bold golden text. 'To be the world leader in…' type of aspirations, you get the gist. In a number of cases this, the organisational chart and a seating plan was the extent of the strategy.

This chapter outlines some of the most common reasons why strategies fail.

3.1 Strategy will flounder without great leadership
Behaviour is contingent on environment. Environment is created, adapted and maintained by leaders. Everything that happens in organisations is down to leadership in some way. Strategy is always going to be a top-down event and so, by definition, it starts at the top. There is more information on leadership - good, bad, mediocre, amazing, appalling and extraordinary - later on in the book.

3.2 Random recruitment
Ask "Why did you pick the individuals in this team to do this job?" and you will get a variety of answers. Some will be ridiculous. Of course, it's easy to say 'get the right people in the right seats on the bus before you set off'; easier to say than do, for sure. However, some appointments I have observed are obvious head scratchers. Professional behavioural climate surveys will help detect mis-steps regarding company promotions.

Problems with teams, problems with collaboration, problems with 'who is supposed to be doing what around here' - all of these will stymie even the wisest (on paper) looking strategy. I have included 'relationship strategy' later in the book; this is another key activity that is rarely performed.

3.3 Nature
Nature rarely gifts us with an effective workplace. Nature will knit together people's reinforcers and their problems with remarkable speed, but an efficient workplace is rarely delivered by leaving things to nature. Nature is good at taking hold of environments, in a bad way,

particularly if people are languishing at the bottom of Maslow's hierarchy of needs. Entropy often takes place in the untended garden, leading to a lack of certainty or predictability and a gradual decline into disorder and dysfunction.

Of course, if you just landed in a new job and have inherited a team with elements of dysfunction it's not nature's fault. Nevertheless, you might still feel somewhat helpless. What's now required will be a considerable amount of discovery, followed by a well-drafted recovery strategy. Discovery can be difficult, especially if you are the new boss. I would suggest that plenty of people will still talk to you, some quite candidly. Just sit down in cafes and have some gentle conversations and develop your relationships and a reliable benchmark on what's happening now. Designing your strategy around the observations will ensure it takes into account people's frames of reference - the everyday reality for them.

3.4 Hierarchy effect

The hierarchy effect is way more influential than you might expect. This is where the team members' value and intelligence are ranked relative to their status or authority and the opinion of the boss ends up being the only valid opinion. It's even got its own acronym: HiPPO (Highest Paid Person's Opinion). What happens is that once the boss's opinion is expressed, then the level of interpersonal risk for everyone else escalates and levels of psychological safety are lowered. Frequently, everyone falls in line, no matter how dumb the decision. Feedback is smothered, and serious problems only get discussed when they finally appear on the bank balance, when it's too late to do anything tangible or effective. Sometimes the leaders get paid off (complete with non-disclosure agreement to censor what really happened.)

So, what is the antidote to this? Well, I like Margaret Mead's advice: "Never doubt that a small group of thoughtful, committed citizens can change the world; indeed, it's the only thing that ever has."

Anyone can get together with a group of like-minded individuals and talk about their problems, worries, ambitions. At some point, enough determination will emerge to change the current path and deliver some energy and reinforcement. For a real change to occur, there usually have to be moments where someone speaks truth to power. The act of speaking truth to power is the very thing that frees you. It allows you to move on to a new enlightened environment, one where you can express yourself with the freedom of knowing you will be valued.

3.5 Micromanagement

Poor leaders in the workplace have an easy and ready source of reinforcement: Micromanagement. They don't have to plan, so there's no need for them to make notes of what they are doing. They can dip in and out of meetings, make knee jerk phone calls and texts, can change their mind multiple times... They are happily in control of the chaos - they are the chaos. All these things are, of course, massively reinforcing for the everyday 'too busy' leader, lost in their own improvised daily lives.

These leaders may not be malicious in their intentions, but the effect they have is no less damaging. The only way to survive this boss-induced chaos is to become a 'sunflower'. A sunflower is a sycophant who is always happy and smiling to the boss but jagged and ugly for the people beneath them in the organisational hierarchy. The 'sunflower effect' can be debilitating for all. It works for the sunflower and, in most places where it thrives, it works really well. In fact, it probably works better than anything else in a workplace that does not encourage feedback or have a desire to seek the truth. A recent productivity study carried out by Hult International Business School examined 28 UK workplaces and found staff who appeared to be "highly engaged". But on closer inspection they were found to be "self-promoters" whose lack of effort pushed down overall business output. It found some very motivated workers - and some who were plainly disgruntled and disaffected. The self-promoters were having a serious debilitating effect on the workers who were trying to enjoy their work and do a contributing job.

3.6 Top loop

This is where a majority of executives become distracted by the excitement of high office, spending way too much of their time with each other. There is plenty of feeding-frenzied optimistic forecasting. No-one below the executives offers up suggestions that the leaders' assumptions may be wrong. There's lots of 'hanging onto something that could never be true but sounded good in the room'.

Top loop does nothing to discourage dysfunctional organisational states. The message is 'we must be upbeat and positive at all times' and this leads to lots of self-congratulatory speeches in conferences. Top loop is typified by large numbers of corporate officers spending small amounts of time (perhaps once a year) with even smaller numbers of factory workers in the name of comradery. Top loop is the slow burning of a genuine workplace culture that could have benefitted everyone. The film about the collapse of Enron, *The Smartest Guys in The Room,* portrayed top loop excellently.

3.7 Artless statements

Occasionally I hear CEOs glibly demanding a genuine open and honest culture in obvious ignorance of what that might mean for themselves and how they would have to adapt their own finely-honed daily behaviours.

A recent fashion in the UK is corporate leaders asking for both efficiency and innovation. Innovation requires experimentation, experimentation requires failure, and failure requires budgets and time. As Simon Sinek said, "Innovation and efficiency are opposites, you can't have both hand in hand. The Wright brothers crashed a lot before they flew."

3.8 A flawed view of reality

Making sure you know what's happening now is a cornerstone of any strategy. One of the greatest barriers to a successful strategy is a flawed frame of reference. There will be performance indicators e.g. bank statements, units delivered, drawings complete, trucks sold etc. I would say that most companies focus on trailing measures:

What happened yesterday, last week, last month, last year etc. Some companies garner feedback from their people and their customers with varying degrees of accuracy. Information comes together to paint a picture and this picture represents the company frame of reference from the perspective of its leaders. I would recommend working hard to verify that your frame of reference is accurate, or risk designing a flawed strategy.

3.9 Distractions

Discover if there are any distracting conversations out there in the workplace. Negative gossip takes up vast amounts of time that could otherwise be put to productive and enjoyable effort. Fifteen years of carrying out opinion surveys in businesses has shown me that there are frequently narratives in the workplace that dominate people's conversations. They change over time, but I would say 80% of the time the distracting narrative centres around one particular boss or one policy (e.g. car parking, timesheets etc). Some examples I recall went on for years and significantly disrupted the projects and companies involved. In most cases the narrative continued for a number of years after the antagonist had gone.

Commonly, when we explain the problem of the distracting narrative to leaders, they tend to dismiss it. I guess it's because a comfortable delusion is better than a cruel truth. For sure, the knowledge workers will be talking about the subject of the day/month/year in their safe places to talk (water cooler, kitchen, pub). No-one can control that narrative without genuinely pursuing it and opening it up for debate, resolution and conclusion. However, if the daily narratives are enthusiastic, work-related conversations then there's a good chance that you are working in a resonant and high-performing workplace, and people are ready and able to focus on role in fulfilling the company's mission.

In this chapter I have summarised a number of barriers to producing or delivering a strategy. Some of these may have resonated with you. In any event I hope I have brought your attention to some potential environment obstacles. The antidote to these barriers is great leadership, more on which in chapter 14.

4.0 What We Hope Is Happening vs What's Really Happening

If the environment is key to behaviour, then having a good read on the current environment is a key step to take. Daniel Kahneman said, "The mind is a machine for jumping to conclusions." When it comes to analysing a workplace environment, there is a good chance of making some inaccurate assumptions. People's opinions are always worth garnering, some may be misinformed, and all will be subjective, but finding out what everyone thinks is paramount. It's what they feel and that should be respected. Combine your knowledge of how people are feeling with some data to get a really accurate read on what's happening. Data is incontrovertible, and a very few people are going to argue against facts (outside politics!).

4.1 What's happening out there?

If you ask a team of knowledge workers to write down 'what's happening out there right now in your business' you will get a lot of generalised labels ("it's great/terrible/fine"), an awful lot of aspirations, a certain amount of 'today's problems', and perhaps some grumbling. You may not get much pinpointed data on what's actually happening out there. It's a hard question to answer; it's the same as asking "What do you want?" It's especially difficult for people to answer properly on the fly. It's almost like we have an 'operational brain' which deals with the localised day-to-day and a rarely used 'strategic brain' that has to be switched on and warmed up before it can be used effectively enough for us to answer the question.

When we run strategy workshops people often walk in with their 'operational, day-to-day head' on. We work hard to create an environment where we can talk about strategic things i.e. openly talk about all possibilities. Despite our attendees having chosen to attend, we frequently observe visible resistance when we ask people to open up from the outset and consider everything. Some people struggle for up to an hour before they can fully move away from operational and into strategic thinking. I guess this demonstrates how hard it must be for one person in a workplace environment trying to introduce a strategic conversation when everyone else is in operational mode.

4.2 Surveys

The good news is that all staff and workforce will willingly spill the beans about what's actually happening out there as long as all the potential threats for punishment have been eradicated. Anonymous surveys are the answer; you don't need me to tell you that you feel completely secure when what you have said cannot be traced back to you. We can all can sense when we have our doubts about whether something is anonymous. A little doubt is all it takes; if real or perceived personal risk is felt, it will negate the chance of garnering any valuable candid opinions.

My advice is that it's not worth trading in the truth for a 'simple to administer' online survey. 'Online survey' means detectable, and the opinions from these surveys are often guarded at best. Getting people in a room with wireless voting buttons and an independent observer to gather the data is the best way of garnering anonymous opinion and asking people to swap transponders before each question is sometimes necessary. Even then, some groups of people still have to be persuaded over time not to just vote what they think the organisation wants them to say.

4.3 The whole truth

The reason it's good to aim for the whole truth first is that the strategy has a better chance of success if it's based it on as much of the whole truth as can be achieved. If it's only based on 50% of the truth, then some of the chances of success just flew away. People moving forward on a strategy with inaccurate assumptions rather that solid facts is a recipe for failure, or some drastic adapting along the way that generates uncertainty. A common organisational pastime is to allow comfortable delusions to dominate the more difficult-to-take feedback or data.

I have seen multiple instances of organisations' leaders inadvertently encouraging staff to hide the truth or to massage the actual data. The leaders in these cases only focused on a small number of financial KPI's, which got all the attention - for good or ill - from the business. Behavioural science will confirm that people will work hard to avoid threats, and this sometimes requires holding off telling the truth. Potential future punishment is usually preferable to actual punishment today.

Some organisations get into trouble by only focusing on a few measures rather than a balance of success factors. Geoff Donaker and Michael Luca said, "If you focus on one metric, expect it to rise, at the expense of the other ones." If the leaders are only focused on talking about sales or money, then it can skew what people prioritise. This is not to be confused with using primary quantities (see 10.1) to provide quick and simple litmus tests.

4.4 The inevitable disappointing feedback

I think a major reason why good quality climate surveys satiate and stop is the inevitable dissatisfaction with the similarities of the results that come back, month in, month out. Things don't improve quickly, especially if all that is happening is the survey. Some people do seem to believe that simply asking the questions will improve workplace behaviours. Leaders need to make the required changes to the workplace environment and, if they do that, the opinions reflected in the surveys will change.

Another potential side-effect of the monthly questionnaire is that people can report that things are getting better just to get the whining bosses off their back. If the survey becomes 'extra work' then it will be treated accordingly. The boss shouting "You lot need to get better" all the time is not a strategy, and hope is not a strategy either. Running a survey is the same as 'weighing yourself at the end of the week'. If it is preceded by 'exercise and a sensible intake of food and drink', it allows you to celebrate your efforts. The improvement occurs during the time in between the weighing. It is what people do day-to-day that delivers the change.

4.5 The solution - an adaptive strategy

All strategies need to have measurement of data on what's happening baked into it. Strategies need ongoing checks and balances, they need a 'how can we avoid some artless fool spoiling this for everyone else' backstop. Finding out the whole truth may well be painful at times but at least it's honest, and it's really the only option on the road to Valhalla. The closer the strategy is to the truth at the outset means the inevitable 'adapting' that will go on over time will be gradual and easier for everyone to implement. Changes to a workplace environment often occur at an excruciatingly slow pace; if the adaptations to the strategy can also be gradual then overall success is more likely. We are building to the adaptive strategy now; a couple more points to make first.

5.0 Culture - What Is It?

5.1 Culture

I use the term 'culture' to mean something overarching, what you would expect to find in 'the railway business' or the 'trucking industry' - very general norms for large groups of people. A general definition of culture will say something like "The day-to-day attitudes, beliefs and behaviour of a particular people or society." I like to stay away from beliefs and attitudes as these are too subjective to be able to work with. Behaviour is what people say and do and is therefore observable and measurable. That means it's something we can more easily work with. (See Appendix B for more detail on how behavioural scientists define behaviours.)

Prior to writing a strategy it's important to allow time for the discovery of the larger 'culture'. The local workplace environments are the keys to what happens in each individual environment and most behaviours are mostly influenced by people's local environments. This fact makes a mockery of the huge global companies that attempt to dictate everyone's unique daily behavioural patterns with no consideration for the local culture: Are they are in China or Brazil? Australia or Portugal? There are some large corporations that try to hold a vice-like grip in an attempt to create a global culture (identical everywhere). The science will tell us that this is an unachievable goal, as it ignores the overwhelming effect of the local environment in people's behaviour. One way or another people find themselves avoiding certain aspects of the attempted corporate handcuffs. These corporations would do well to realise that their desired outputs could still be delivered productively in a different way in each of the separate individual environments across the globe. Remove the handcuffs – allow people to perform effectively.

5.2 Environment

The environment is the immediate location of a person, be it in their office, living room, their car; it's the place and the people in that place; it is wherever behaviours are occurring and includes the other people in that location. A person's behaviour is mostly driven by the consequences that have followed their behaviour (or similar behaviours) in the past. The local environment will dictate the consequences people experience or believe they may experience following each behaviour. Small changes in environment can result in significant changes in the behaviour of an individual. The environment influences our behaviour and we influence the environment. Dr B.F. Skinner said that "humans operate on their environment" and I like to refer back to that model. You might say to yourself "I am walking into our office and I have just begun to affect this environment, one way or another."

Imagine an office full of people. Take one person out of the office and replace them with a different person - the environment has just changed. The significance of the change will be different depending on who left and who came in. Taking some selected dominant characters out of an environment can significantly change everything for the people left in the room.

6.0 The 80/20 rule

The 80/20 rule was first put forward by Vilfredo Pareto. He was an Italian economist (born in Paris) who famously observed that "20% of my pea plants contain 80% of the peas." He went on to discover many situations that supported his 80/20 rule, starting with statistics on the distribution of wealth. He found that in the UK, 20% of the population held 80% of the wealth. He looked at other European countries and discovered the same finding. People have since attempted to find a mathematical reason for this empirical law with little persuasive success.

Many scholars and writers have talked about 80/20 over the years, the most prominent (and successful) being Richard Koch. He has written many books, including *The 80/20 Principle*. Many baffling statistics, some might say coincidences, appear in his book. Here are some of his top choices:

- 20% of your time delivers 80% of your profits
- 20% of the people are responsible for 80% of the progress
- 20% of causes lead to 80% of the results
- You will wear 20% of your clothes 80% of the time
- 20% of professional athletes win 80% of the prizes
- 20% of the cities in the UK are home to 80% of the population
- 20% of your carpets get 80% of the wear
- 20% of burglars will make off with 80% of the loot

He said, "The amazing thing about the 80/20 principle is that very few things matter at all; but those that do, matter enormously." Why is this principle mentioned here? Look again at the first three items on the list above: All strategy. The difficulty with the 80/20 rule is that it is a counterintuitive imbalance, it feels wonky. This rule also says that people blunder all the time when it comes to how they utilise their time at work; 80% of time being almost completely wasted on activities that do not create wealth or the conditions for wealth-creation by others. Leaders could work to ascertain if 80% of their results truly derive from 20% of their people's activities. There is the potential for an extremely desirable advantage to be discovered.

There is a mistaken belief amongst some that "I am a good person and a hard worker; therefore all my daily efforts will lead to good things." But without analysis this mindset is dominated by cognitive biases supporting 'what makes me feel good'. In fact, observation and analysis of actual daily behaviours is the only way to detect which of your efforts are bringing the desirable things.

There is a good chance that most leaders spend 80% of their time on the things they find personally reinforcing, but which might not be what they should be doing for the benefit of their organisation, its people and their customers. I would expect most people will not know which 20% of what they do derives 80% of the value. This is a conundrum that requires observation, data and an honest approach about the what, who, where, when, why of the daily behaviours of leaders.

Back in November 2018 I asked our local farmer about the multicoloured
stained backs of the sheep in his fields. He explained that he ties bags
of dye onto the chest of the ram and this rubs off onto the back of
the ewes, telling him when they have been 'tupped'. I asked him how
accurate this was as an indicator of sheep copulation and he said,
"It works about 80% of the time."

Section B: Writing A Strategy
7.0 Strategy and Behavioural Science

In order to write a strategy that has a good chance of working, the strategy writers have to be open and honest with themselves. They must have the freedom to brainstorm a lot of ideas - covering all sorts of possibilities - and get a lot of potential obstacles out in the open so that the whole stew can be considered and analysed. The goal is to ultimately produce something that everyone genuinely thinks has a chance of success. Often people will say 'oh yes, this'll work' until pressed more specifically. Initially, optimism and impatience tend to emerge naturally. The trick is finding a strategy for your current reality in a relaxed and calm way, without seeming pessimistic.

A strategy that is flexible requires frequent reviews, quarterly, perhaps even monthly at the start. If the review of your strategy is at three months and it looks like the end result was overly ambitious, it might need adapting. The science says that it's better to be working in a discretionary environment aiming for a lower goal than working in an aversive environment for a doubtful higher goal or an impossible goal. In fact, the only way the original higher goal could ever be achieved would be in an environment delivering lots of discretion. Creating this resonant, open, positive mood requires that no-one feels under a threat of failure. If this is not the case, the dissonance produces a paradox of gigantic proportions which cannot be overcome.

At the start of the movie *Butch Cassidy and the Sundance Kid* the Sundance Kid has been accused of cheating at cards. Offended by the accusation, Butch and Sundance want to leave but have to save face. Sundance tells his friend, "If he invites us to stay, then we'll go... He's got to invite us to stick around." It's a counterintuitive request, and it's exactly like this when it comes to recovering loss in a strategy. The only way to achieve it is in a positive environment and so leaders have to work out how to create this. Simply demanding a result is easy by comparison. Well, it is easy to be demanding, it is easy to say the words out loud; getting the right result by simply demanding it is of course, unlikely. The right result requires the right environment; creating the right environment is the wise and compassionate move.

8.0 The Adaptive Strategy

The Dalai Lama famously said, "If scientific analysis were conclusively to demonstrate certain claims in Buddhism to be false, then we must accept the findings of science and abandon those claims." He is talking about adapting to new information appearing along the journey. It doesn't matter how much or how thorough the planning has been, things happen that divert the course of the plan. Adjustments have to be made along the way and frequent reviews need to take place to see if the strategy is still producing the confidence the original plan had.

There is no right or wrong decision; there is a decision to do either A or B and then there is a result or effect, over time. You never will know what would have happened if you had picked the other option at that time. Some would say the most important aspect of this conundrum is being decisive, quickly toss a coin and make a move!

There are numerous models of strategic plans out there, part 6 of Max McKeown's The Strategy Book summarises most of them adequately. There are some very simple models out there e.g. Deming's PDCA (plan, do, check, act), I prefer OPDCA (observe, plan, do, check, act) as it supports the need to truly find out what's happening right now before moving to the next step. The logical extension of this simple beginning might be to develop an adaptive plan.

8.1 An adaptive strategy

It's fair to assume that any strategic plan will veer off in the early stages of its life, if not on day one. If that's the case, then the plan needs to have change baked into it. A logical process then might be:

1. Observe what's happening now
2. Write a simple plan for change (What? Who? Where? When? Why? How?)
3. Roll out and test the plan
4. Survey for feedback, analyse and adapt the plan accordingly
5. Iterate

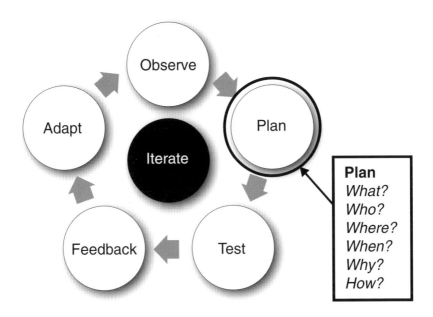

It's worth remembering that 'what's happening now' reflects all things in the environment that are reinforcing the current behaviours (for good or ill). Effective change of any sort will require the identification of these reinforcers and a plan that is designed to outweigh the current reinforcers, the current 'day to day norms'. People don't naturally resist change, however they do resist 'the perception of loss' and this resistance is what commonly emerges when someone tries to introduce change into a workplace environment.

The goal is usually the creation of some kind of a high-performing team that will deliver great things. In a real high-performing team there's a little bit of chaos but a compensating glut of creativity that outweighs the uncertainty caused by the chaos. Changing from a traditional 'locked down hierarchical' scenario to one that unlocks the potential of all the people is a mammoth journey. Easily requested, very difficult to achieve from a traditional 'top down' culture. High levels of performance are always possible, but the workplace environment of the high-performing team will not reinforce mistrust or bureaucracy, so dysfunctional behaviours are starved and die.

The adaptive plan grows over time; it starts with a few stabs at What? Who? Where? When? Why? and How? The cognitive effect of iterating and growing a strategy can be incredibly reinforcing, especially when it gets to the 'how is everyone going to work together to deliver these elements of this strategy?' part.

I would recommend that each member of the team who will be writing the strategy first write their own personal strategic plan. Doing this will provide a backdrop to what's to come.

9.0 Designing A Strategic Plan

The strategy model outlined below can be adapted for all areas of business and life. Because it is helpful to design a personal strategic plan - one written by a single person rather than by a team - before embarking on more wide-ranging strategies, this chapter will use a personal strategy as a model.

Behavioural science states that behaviour is contingent on the environment it operates on. Performance is a product of behaviours delivering results within a given environment. So, your plan should consider both results and behaviours.

First consider your desired objectives in line with the model - What? Why? Who? When? Where? These questions are antecedents, acting as prompts to help focus your strategy. Then, describe which behaviours will contribute to these results – i.e. the How?
Your strategic plan then could be your answers to these questions:

Results (What)
1. What is it that you want to achieve?
2. Why do you want this goal?
3. Who else is involved in the realisation of this goal?
4. When is the result required?
5. Where will this be happening?

Behaviours (How)
1. How will you ensure you have satisfied all the 'W's?
2. How will the required people work together to achieve this goal?
3. How and when will you test to see if it's working?

I am going to lean some more on Dr Michael Porter's work for this section. For a personal strategy, you are unlikely to be working towards goals in a vacuum, and having a good understanding of yourself, your boundaries and your allies will help you design a better strategy. Once you have listed your results and behaviours, test your responses to see if your stated results and behaviours fit Dr Porter's recommendation for what should be in a strategy. Consider:

1. What is your unique value proposition? That is, what combination of skills, talents and experiences can only you bring?
2. How is what you could offer different to what's happening now?
3. What would you be willing to give up in order to achieve your goals?
4. What have you decided not to do?
5. Which of the activities you've mentioned fit together and reinforce each other?
6. Where is the continual improvement in realising this strategy going to come from?

Your next steps:
1. Write down the new 2nd draft of your strategic plan
2. List the obvious barriers to success, what's happening now that will probably try to kill your new strategy?
3. Consider how to overcome the barriers: Who must you ask for support?

I have been testing this process out with some willing subjects. It was a discovery in every case, and an enjoyable one at that. It may look and feel a little clunky, especially as a redrafting process is required, but it works, every time.

Starting to learn the strategy process here is also very valuable. It is likely that people will initially be interested in a strategy for themselves, and it is easier to consider oneself for a first attempt rather than one a team or the wider business. Getting confident with the process is a key part of the exercise. Putting personal strategy front and centre also helps with understanding the skills and talents on offer to support the 'overall mission', as well as bringing any barriers to light.

In my company, we have a mission to do 'cool things with cool people in cool places'. Members of the Hollin team can be heard asking "Is this cool things with cool people in cool places?" Sometimes there is a resounding "no" and sometimes a "yes." It's a simple litmus test to see if we have wandered off our desired path.

9.1 The relationship adaptive strategy

Every coaching session at some point throws up a relationship problem of some kind. Either a boss, a peer or a subordinate that is causing our coaching client an upsetting problem or, in a lot of cases, 'driving them bonkers'! Working through the What/Who/Where/When/Why/How process can, at times, get emotional. I wrote a book called *Power Coaching* and it contains many ideas for what to do about typical dysfunction in the various relationships that one would have at work.

For work-related strategies to be really successful, the workplace relationships need to be trusting, robust and resonant. The first iteration of any strategy might need to focus on the key relationships needed to create an environment that will have a good chance of delivering the 'how'. This is usually achieved by having a specific relationship session with the team. The leader might say things like 'we are where we are' or 'let's draw a line under it'. If the elephant in the room does not emerge then you might have to seek professional help.

A relationship strategy is going to have to deal with compromise, because the team need to focus on the overall mission and reflect on the best way to get there. People in the team may have to accept things they don't like for the greater good. Being sympathetic to this is a good frame of mind with which to enter the room. This is not a place for winning the argument, this is the place where you win the whole game.

10.0 An Adaptive Strategy –
Is This Going To Be Possible For You?

In this chapter, I will explore some ideas to help you refine aspects of your strategy, including measuring success and some ideas around reviewing your goals.

Of course, I could say, "Follow this path, here is a process, start at step one and by the time you get to step ten all your strategy mysteries will be solved and ready to enact." My difficulty is that I have no view of your workplace. I have no idea what's possible in your world. This is why examples of other people's strategies are generally of little help. Every time we run a strategy workshop, people say "Can you give us some real examples?" When we do, we get feedback saying, "This isn't us," or "This would not work in my company" etc.
Nevertheless, I have included some examples of strategies in Appendix A.

10.1 Measuring success with primary quantities

Is there a primary quantity in your business/project? Something that everything else hangs off? If you are writing a book, then words on a page could be your primary quantity. If you are building a large concrete viaduct then 'amount of concrete poured' could be the primary quantity. If you are selling services, then 'work booked' could be your primary quantity. The benefit of focusing on primary quantities is that these can be used as the litmus test along the way, the quick and simple thing that warns you to quickly look in detail at something.

My plea to 'keep things simple' gets ignored by most people; it's way too tempting and reinforcing to try to think of everything and write it all down. I often see meeting room walls festooned with flip chart scribblings. I see people making copious notes in meetings and wonder, when do they read these notes? If they just sat back and listened instead could they take the information in here and now? Quantity kills quality everywhere. If you can set up a shortcut to 'what's actually happening' then you can glance at it along the way, that's all I am saying.

A word of warning: It's no good having a primary quantity if the primary quantity trumps everything else and delivers overall failure. Sometimes people can set up their own 'primary quantity' that works against some of the other organisational desired outputs. One company I worked with had a team whose stated strategic target was to make as many successful sales trips as possible. Unfortunately, the team figured out that they only had to sell small amounts on each of these trips for the company to reward them, so they visited all the nice destinations that would certainly buy a little instead of visiting the less desirable cities where they may have sold a lot.

Wealth creators sometimes use this primary measure and then skew their reported results to satisfy it, more often to avoid actual or perceived punishment rather than for personal gain (despite my anecdote above). The antidote to this corporate phenomenon is frequent and honest feedback.

10.2 What? So what? Now what?

If you can describe what it is that you want and don't want, can you then describe it in simple terms? Describe it in such simple terms that everyone involved will understand it? High-performing teams are always looking for improvements in some way, so baking into the strategy an incentive for people to take appropriate risks is paramount. Leaders can encourage people to innovate but this does not occur naturally on demand. People will need encouragement for taking risks and this must always be supported with budgets for them to use.

There are many workplace circumstances that throw up fleeting opportunities. High-performing teams recognise these and build on them. It is the entrepreneurial spirit, the enjoyment of building a business, a team, an idea or a strategy. My old company use to call this 'leveraging diversity': He has a sand pit, she has a quarry, let's buy some cement and make concrete!

I like the simplicity of 'what, so what, and now what'. It's a shorthand that can be used to develop a strategy and also adapt the strategy along the way. Most information in workplaces is not weak or hidden - it is evident, right there in front of everyone. Most operations can be questioned; it is soothing to question something and discover that it's the right thing to do after all. That process itself creates a feedback-rich environment, and that feedback produces a reinforcing value within the workplace. Frequent, honest feedback also generates the discretionary effect and, as they say, that is where the fun and the money is.

10.3 Choosing scientific strategic measurements

Behavioural science indicates that any goal has to be seen as eminently achievable by the performer. This is the only way to create an environment where the performer will be inspired to deliver discretionary effort - going the extra mile to exceed the initial goal. Dr Aubrey Daniels has written numerous excellent books on discretionary effect, where people get to choose high-performance. For knowledge workers to achieve such high performance they have to be working in a workplace environment that supports it. In part, this means using appropriate measurements.

When it comes to individual measures, choosing the right one is a key component to achieving genuine high performance. The initial bar has to be low enough for the performer to believe they can hurdle it from the outset. An adaptive strategy will encourage review and adjustment, so there needs to be no fear that the initial goal might be too low. The temptation, however, is often to set something 'challenging' and that sometimes means 'impossible' from the performer's perspective. Doing this creates aversion and that's a bad thing!

A number of years ago I was in a debate with someone over setting a contract period. The protagonist was saying, "We need to make the contract period 18 weeks, then if they complete in 22 weeks, we will still be happy as that's the actual time period we want." My argument was for us to be honest and set the period at the 22-week time period we want. Perhaps then pay an early completion bonus for every early week they delivered. I argued that this offer is the only way to create discretionary effort: The bar is low enough to jump over and the supplier could get a nice bonus out of this too. This would have been the smart way forward. Predictably, I was overruled.

Setting the bar too high at the start meant the contractors delivered 'just enough' performance, resulting in a late completion and a bucket full of claims.

10.4 Motivating factors

It is a fallacy that setting a 'too high' goal will encourage people to attempt to achieve it. We all like to embark on a journey we believe is eminently achievable. It's the only way (barring blind luck) to get there early. We are now in the area of psychology relating to 'what people find motivating'. If you were to take a journey through the works of Douglas McGregor (Theory X & Y), Freddie Herzberg (Motivator-Hygiene Theory), Abraham Maslow (The Hierarchy of Needs), and many others you will learn that high motivation is an environmental matter. It is important to identify the dominant creator and sustainer of the particular local environment as they are going to be the most influential performer.

B.F. Skinner's work on applied behaviour analysis indicates that antecedents (attempts to get behaviours going) will have only limited influence on prompting or maintaining behaviour. He noted that behaviours are influenced primarily by the immediate consequences perceived and then received by the performer following the behaviour, whether those are pleasant, unpleasant or neutral. Skinner's discovery underlines the fundamental truth that in order to get high performance, an environment has to be created to support high performance. Workplace environments frequently undermine high performance, often through attrition; knowledge workers are often so busy ticking bureaucratic boxes that getting the work done is a secondary goal.

If a change strategy is desired in an existing workplace environment, then step one is (as always) to find out what's happening now. Analysing and understanding the current sets of antecedents and consequences is paramount if a scientific approach is to be successful with a new strategy.

So, what do people like? People like recognition and being appreciated, in a genuine and sincere way, and neither of these acts costs any money. Of course, they do require someone's time and attention. Recognition (often a simple 'thanks for doing that thing') and being appreciated are the key elements of a high-performing team workplace environment, along with a number of other things that don't overtly 'cost money' but do take up someone's time.

Organisations frequently look to bribe people with bonuses into doing productive work, but most knowledge workers don't need to be bribed. High-performing, motivated knowledge workers will deliver time and time again if their workplace environment supports it. This does not necessitate spending sums of money to achieve, just knowledge and an understanding of how to remove the barriers to a great, productive environment.

The good leaders always recognise the value of genuine recognition. I am not saying bonuses are bad, as there can be great joy in receiving an unexpected bonus. The benefits of variable bonuses massively outweigh the traditional 'expected' annual bonus which may even be demotivating if it's any less in value than last year's bonus. You might say that an unexpected bonus is the only true bonus. Great companies allow their leaders discretion when it comes to spot bonuses; they have a pot of money to use as they see fit which is great for everyone (well, the 20% that get 80% of the bonuses!)

Why do people work? For money? Herzberg said that "People work to avoid the money stopping anytime." Behavioural science calls this 'negative reinforcement', i.e. living under the threat of a loss. Herzberg's research suggests that people work best because they want to enjoy the activity. Some organisations look on incentivisation as purely a money thing e.g. if you do that, we will give you this money in return. From a motivational perspective it could be argued that it's a misuse of bonuses and salaries. I would suggest that it's unwise to mess with anything that disrupts the 'discretionary effort' of the majority of the happy wealth creators in the company - find out what's important to each of them.

10.5 So, is this going to be possible for you?

It's always possible to achieve something. If you view the more pioneering suggestions within this chapter as 'impossible in your world' then perhaps have a think about strategies that would be mostly within your sphere of control. The personal plan and the relationship plan can be devised in the comfort of your own home, away from any of the threats you might perceive. In the words of Peter Gabriel: "Don't give up."

11.0 90-Day Strategic Plan

This kind of strategy is useful for a new business or the reorganisation of an existing one. In my experience it is commonly adopted by a leader starting a job in a new organisation, perhaps taking over a new job of high office (a new CEO perhaps). As always, a detailed and accurate assessment of the current state of the business will be required as soon as possible.

The discovery phase will generally consist of meeting as many people as possible in order to get a feel for the organisation and its people and customers. This can be enhanced by carrying out a comprehensive independent climate survey; getting a neutral party to design and roll out a survey (using anonymous voting pads if possible). It's always important to validate all the findings with selected interviews. This kind of benchmark is also valuable going forward for the new leader, as they can rerun the survey every three months and track progress.

'There's a new boss in town' is often supported by senior leadership undertaking strategic or collaboration workshops, and the use of independent consultants and executive coaches. The new leader may well take advantage of the incumbent leadership team to assist in writing the strategy going forward. Using independent help during this phase can enhance the fact-finding; turning over all the rocks and cataloguing what's under them in order to speed up discovery and secure the desired new strategy.

12.0 Simple Balanced Scorecards

A balanced scorecard provides a quick graphical overview of how a team is performing in key areas. Balanced scorecards are designed to be displayed prominently to help develop, communicate and measure the success of the strategy.

The primary reasons to use a balanced scorecard are:

1. To ensure the team understand and agree the strategy for the project, organisation or business.
2. To measure performance and adapt the measures if needed.
3. For the delivery team to celebrate their successes as they occur.

12.1 The adaptive strategy and the behavioural balanced scorecard

A behavioural balanced scorecard is a method of recording and sharing data that allows a team to measure their own performance using a combination of results and behaviours. This scorecard fits beautifully with the Adaptive Strategy. The sets of desired behaviours may be more complex and obviously will involve more people than the personal plan, but the science can still be applied and be successful. If a leader can create the workplace environment that will deliver the right suite of day-to-day behaviours, there is a good chance that sustainable success will follow.

The scorecard should measure a small number of key behaviours over the period of the scorecard (commonly one year). These behaviours will evolve and change over the period of the scorecard as required. Measuring these 'shaped behaviours' will provide the performers with a considerably better idea of 'how' the strategic goal is to be achieved than the standard 'end result' element of most common business measures (KPI's, goals, objectives etc). Measuring performance using simple, unambiguous behaviours means that the performers are much more likely carry out those key behaviours. Successful scorecards create buy-in from those performers who are key to its success, i.e. the value-adding contributors to the organisation. A successful scorecard will sustain interest over time, over many years in some cases. The purpose of a behavioural balanced scorecard is to describe and share the adaptive strategy and goals with the performers, and to enable the acknowledgement and celebration of all movement in the right direction.

12.2 Peer pressure

Research on peer pressure indicates that it is a much stronger force in driving behaviour than many of us instinctively feel it would be. It is often driven by a combination of 'fear of missing out' (FOMO) and 'fear of other people's opinions'. In the early stages of running a balanced scorecard it's common for people to resist certain elements of it. Some might feel threatened by it; they could question the measures. Some might question the data or doubt the purpose of this scorecard.

Some may assume it's going to be just the same as all the past initiatives and some may simply ignore it. It's important for the scorecard administrator to continue to relentlessly publish the data from that month and publicise the scorecards. Over time, each dissenter realises that this scorecard actually is different. When people eventually realise that the stated purpose of the scorecard - to describe and share the strategy and goals with the performers - is real, they relax into it and join in.

12.3 Use existing baseline data

As previously mentioned, I am dismayed, but not surprised, when I observe very high aspirational targets being set for future performance without taking into account the current performance of the team or organisation. It is a common mistake for leaders (or corporate departments) to view next year from the security of their own happy bubble. Setting targets for next year should be an opportunity to review the strategy and adapt it to take account of what happened last year. Ideally, it is an opportunity to enable teams to be involved in setting their own targets. If the leaders can be honest about all the current data, there is a good chance that a successful shaping plan can be designed. (Shaping is explained in Appendix B)

You cannot make informed decisions unless you have all the data regarding what is really happening every day. It takes a lot of time to get to a position where you have all the correct data, but it is a vital first step.

12.4 Be patient

A long term effective shaping plan may mean achieving half your desired goal this year and the final half next year. Major cultural change can take many years. I am frequently asked, "How long do you think it takes to change the culture in a company?" My reply is always: "Depending on the size of the company, three to five years."

We see many unsuccessful short-term initiatives that have attempted to create large sustainable changes in less than one year. It's an example of the classic 'up and down the elastic zone' failed initiative, driven partly by impatience and partly by a lack of understanding of just how long sustainable change takes. Overly ambitious time scales for change also reflect a lack of understanding by leaders of the current consequences supporting the workplace environment. There will be thousands of reinforcers maintaining the current workplace environment, and every single one of them will be defended if threatened. Change takes time.

12.5 Stretch goals

I have seen stretch goals misused many times. The purpose of a well-conceived stretch goal is to offer an opportunity for the team to overachieve. This means the team can make up for underachieving goals and still succeed. In the real world, organisations are subject to all kinds of disruptive elements; markets change, unforeseen problems occur, even the weather can disrupt your plans.

For scoring, I like the process of having a 13-point scale, where step 10 is the genuine desired goal. This stretch goal facility allows people to overachieve on some measures, knowing they are going to inevitably underachieve on some others. The '13-point stretch goal' scale allows the performers some flexibility and relief from threat of failure. It is also wise to change under-performing measures and adapt them accordingly. After all, what's the point of spending the rest of the year looking at something that has already failed? You got it wrong but continuing to focus on it won't help. Replace it with something else: This is about adapting to win the overall race.

12.6 Leading and trailing measures

The most common measures in business are 'trailing' measures. They are the results of what's already happened. Trailing measures commonly include 'profit', 'overhead', 'injury rates', 'customer surveys', 'operational results', 'power usage', 'attrition rates' etc. These are the measures after the fact, at month and year end; you are reading the bank statement and it shows a reflection of what you did last month. Trailing measures are the 'rear view mirror' measures.

Leading measures are more likely to be behaviours. What do you see looking forward? Do people turn up on time, respond in a timely fashion, set clear expectations, seek early feedback, coach their direct reports, publish survey results, publish data on their own behaviours? These are the dynamic measures, the 'what's happening now' measures, the plate-spinning measures, the wealth-creating measures. If you are successful at these things, you already know that the bank statement will be a pleasure to read before it arrives. By using carefully pinpointed leading measures, people will know which individual and team behaviours will lead to success. Leading measures aim to identify and measure the things we need to be doing 'more of' or 'less of' to achieve improved performance.

Both leading and trailing measures are equally important. The leading measures are the 'food intake and exercise' measures and the trailing measure is 'the weighing session at the end of the week'. Celebration occurs when the trailing measures say this week's goal has been reached (or exceeded).

Many teams are only measured on final end-of-year results; pass or fail. There are a number of downsides to this, the most obvious being that if a measure has failed in the early months of the year then the performers may no longer consider it important. They believe they have failed, that they cannot win on this measure. They are left to do the best they can with what's left to achieve, leading to a demoralised team who are not performing at their best. It's another great reason to operate an adaptive strategy within an enlightened scorecard.

12.7 Celebrating success

Celebrating success is a simple-sounding but much misunderstood key element of a successful scorecard. It is paramount that the delivery team get to choose what they deem celebrating looks like. Traditionally-led teams commonly suffer from receiving too much attention when things go wrong and too little attention when things go well. 'Extinction' (where people expect to receive reinforcement for what they do but don't get any) causes a lot of frustration and kills discretionary effort very effectively.

Avoiding extinction is a key feature of high-performing teams; it goes hand in hand with removing uncertainty. If everyone in the team is certain about their part in the success of the team then it maximises the chances of achieving that success. It's great to celebrate, especially if it's properly done and everyone agrees how it will be done. It works well combined with great leaders who recognise good performance as it occurs, in a skilled and personal way.

12.8 Summary

Here is a quick summary of what I'd recommend when deciding what to measure and how to do it so that the people doing the work don't feel that it's just another box to tick:

- Carefully choose a small number of primary quantities
- Select the key behaviours
- Use a simple scorecard to build and then monitor the strategy
- Let the wealth-creators write the scorecard, unmolested
- Keep it simple, adapt when necessary, publish relentlessly, let it develop traction on its own

BMT Scorecards is a free downloadable Hollin book from **www.hollin.co.uk/shop**

Section C: Contributory Factors
13.0 Strategic, Tactical, Operational

I spoke about 'operational brain' and 'strategic brain' in chapter
4. I want to open this concept up further. This book focuses on
strategy, so we have not ventured far into either tactical planning
or operational detail.

The terms 'strategic', 'tactical' and 'operational' are from the military.
'Strategic' is defined as the decision where a nation or nations decide
to go to war. 'Tactical' would be the decisions made regarding which
parts of the military machine are going to do what. 'Operational'
would be the day-to-day battle decisions. The feedback gained
regularly from operations either confirms or puts doubt on the efficacy
of the strategy, and points to what needs adapting.

13.1 Strategic

Many years ago, I worked for US Marine General Jack Sheehan.
He used to say, "When I was Supreme Commander at NATO, I had
a million people working for me, most of them in 'operational'
mode. If I jumped down into 'operational' that would have made
a million and one in 'operational' and no-one in 'strategic'. Does that
sound dumb to you?" I most certainly admired his ability to stay in
strategic and never get dragged down into the detail. I now admire
his ability to avoid stepping in and solving a problem. One or two
searching questions followed by a "Let me know how you get on"
used to irritate me, but I believe I understand the wisdom in his
behaviour now. The seeds of effective delegation and responsibility
germinate when leaders allow people to do their own jobs - in fact,
insist on it at every turn.

It can be true that the day-to-day throws up lots of interesting problems
and situations and they can be very tempting. The successful leader
realises this and learns how to be a strategic leader and stays in that box
despite the temptations; more strains of "let me know how you get on."

The interesting problems that crop up day-to-day can be noted and added to the list of subjects for the next coaching session.

13.2 Tactical

This is the middle management role, the crucial bridge between the operational business and the strategic leader, board of directors etc. In large organisations, the job of the people in this layer is to figure out how to make the strategy work in the various divisions of the company.

13.3 Operational

This layer within the business is where most of the direct wealth-creators are. Most of the folks in strategic and tactical are a cost overhead, whereas most of the folks in operational do tangible things for the company. This is where the work occurs.

13.4 Stay in your lane

When the various officers within the organisation stick to their ideal zone of involvement - whether strategic, tactical, or operational - business is usually more effective. Leaders often struggle to stay in 'strategic' and dive into the detail. Similarly, managers often struggle to stay in 'tactical', as there is a constant temptation to carry out operational work, especially for those people promoted from the shop floor. There are lots of behavioural reasons why this happens, but it's mostly because 'immediate reinforcing consequences' abound down in the weeds.

For leaders, staying in strategic is hard. It requires focus and cannot be improvised. The leaders are there to stay focused and get the strategy right, and this requires strength of character. Great leaders have already learned how hard it is to see things, know the answers and still say nothing. Great leaders know that the hard-learned lessons had a great impact on their understanding of leadership. I am not saying that great leaders will stand by idly and watch someone fail. I am saying that an open question here and there is about all the interfering great leaders do.

14.0 Creating The Environment That Delivers The Strategy

Execution of the strategy occurs in the workplace; the workplace environment is created and maintained by the leadership. What would you expect from a great leader? For balance, what would a poor leader do?

The two stereotypes are extreme, however the great leaders I have encountered display most of the attributes on the left-hand side of the list below. Likewise, the poor leaders I have encountered displayed most of the attributes listed on the right. I have an idea of the proportion of these character types I have observed over the years and it weighs more on the poor leader than the good one, sadly.

Great Leader	Poor Leader
Seeks out, disrupts and dismantles cliques	Maintains cliques or is unaware of them
Recognises that the leadership team, together, must decide the strategy	Carries the strategy around in their head
Is known for being calm and considered	Is susceptible to knee-jerk reactions
Works to improve quality of all relationships; is collaborative	Uses divides between executives as a source of control
People have a problem	People are a problem
Recognises that problems are too complex for any one person to have all the answers	Asserts their need to be right
Is always makings observations about patterns and routines	Reacts and wants action when there is discomfort/ uncertainty

Great Leader	Poor Leader
Makes sure supervisors/junior managers are always in charge of day-to-day activities	Expects the senior managers to know all the details
Focuses on 'how do we get the work done?'	Focuses on 'understanding the status'
Focuses on managing the environment: Works to creates the conditions for desired behaviours	Focuses on managing people and their perceived attitudes
Has a simple plan. Is always working on a better plan (one informed by feedback so people are acting on reality)	Strategies are 150 slides long, and the strategy changes context every year
Books time for thinking, always has gaps between meetings, encourages 'white space' scheduling	Is busy - 'back to back' meetings
Always allows time for others to catch up; is calm and patient	Vents their frustrations; is impatient and emotional
Makes it safe for people to reveal the truth	Inadvertently creates a chronic lack of honesty
Spends time looking for opportunities (wealth creation)	Spends time on allocating blame (loss aversion)
Is humble in both victory and defeat	Gloats in victory and whines in defeat
You feel safe talking to them, in fact you feel inspired	You feel unsafe talking to them, in fact it's scary
Will ask you what you think	Will tell you what to do

Great Leader	Poor Leader
Will give you feedback on your behaviour and it will feel energising	Will tell you what they think, and it will feel punishing
Will be enquiring what's happening and asking who needs help	Will be looking at spreadsheets and RAG reports, and demanding improvements in the numbers
People are confident and comfortable asking them for help	People are unlikely to ask them for advice
People feel secure, less likely to arse-cover/keep secrets	Emails are rife, copied to everyone, cultural arse-covering is the norm
Will talk earnestly and openly about employee safety	Employee safety will not be mentioned
Will talk about the importance of a coaching culture	Will not talk about 'touchy feely' stuff. Will use the phrase 'touchy feely'
Will deal artfully with what they see as poor performance in their team	Will either ignore what they see as poor performance or deal with it artlessly
Will ask "How can I help simplify things for you?"	Will make demands, which will be received in silence
Will take bad news with sensitivity and understanding for the messenger	Will be emotional in meetings when things go wrong
Has a strong and caring leadership style	Uses management by exception
Encourages all leaders to ask for dissenting opinions	Will not ask for dissenting opinions

Great Leader	Poor Leader
Will be generous, trusts people with discretionary spending, funds new ideas	Will hold the purse strings unduly tightly, discretionary spend will be very small
Understands the likelihood of cognitive bias and encourages different perspectives	Is recklessly blind to cognitive bias when making decisions
Knows the team well enough to notice when personal issues are weighing heavily	Doesn't really know all the team, plays favourites
Stays in 'adult' in team meetings, avoids publicly criticising others	Can be sarcastic in team meetings regarding team members
Is discreet, can be trusted with sensitive information, so people are happy to disclose	Can be reckless with private or sensitive information about people given in confidence
In large group situations makes sure they spend time with as many people as possible, not just peers and seniors	Sticks to their favourites in large group situations
Will readily apologise	Does not readily apologise
Understands the concept of discretionary effort and recognises where it is occurring in the business.	High performance is a permanent expectation; "That's what they get paid for"

15.0 More On Stereotypes

I asked a large group of people to list the characteristics of people they have encountered in their past and present. It's not surprising that they generalise into quite a small number of stereotypes. This is extremely subjective, and definitely not scientific.

The list below contains stereotypes of some folks who are in some way flawed and therefore unlikely to create a winning strategy.
If you find yourself with one of these characters in charge, watch out! I have chosen a name type followed by labels based on some of the characteristics appropriate for each stereotype:

1. The Dictator
   a. Uses tyranny to control, divide and rule
   b. Does not solicit feedback
   c. Does not ask for dissenting opinions
   d. Gets very aggressive if challenged
   e. Their credo is - management by exception
   f. It's hard to predict their responses
   g. Not as rare as you might hope
   h. Their success is based on the allure, perception and temptation of power
   i. The people they gather around them are submissive and fearful
   j. Often seen by their masters as someone who is going to 'sort things out and deliver'

2. The Ditherer
   a. An indecisive boss who is fearful of their masters
   b. It's trouble getting them to decide anything
   c. They keep their head down, never looking over the parapet
   d. Observes failure and says nothing
   e. Hears bullying and says nothing
   f. They're just running out time to their pension
   g. They don't call you back, or respond to your emails
   h. Dresses well, nice car
   i. Loves the detail, got promoted into this job after being so good at knowing everything in their last job

3. The Leash-Strainer

a. An overly-ambitious leader who wants to take all the credit themselves
b. Aims to be the smartest person in the room
c. Gets to the answers first at the expense of everyone else
d. Can be likeable and charismatic
e. Joins all the clubs, societies, anything the company will fund
f. Gets extra unnecessary qualifications
g. Always in the photograph at the awards ceremonies
h. Does nothing in between meetings but is a quick thinker and retorts well during meetings
i. Is loud and confident, sometimes wrong, but mostly unchallenged
j. Is unreliable, will push you under a bus if necessary
k. Charismatic and liked by their leaders, but disliked by peers
l. Identifies as a coach, yet no-one wants coaching from them!
m. Can easily get falsely scored as an A player

4. The Old Guard

a. The older boss whose pension is in sight, so doesn't make any decisions or changes
b. Talks about retirement all the time, everyone knows the details of their pension deal
c. The reality for them is that "it's always been this way"
d. Wants and gets an easy life from bosses in return for supporting votes and supressing the troops
e. Rationalises, in favour retaining a position of safety for themselves
f. Is still fearful of loss of their pension at the last minute
g. Is a competent enough person simply unable to face the real or perceived pressure of high office

5. The Nice Neighbour

a. Earnest, usually very technically qualified
b. Lacks interpersonal skills and doesn't do 'pastoral care' for team members
c. Is a responder - "my door is always open"
d. Rarely takes the initiative

e. Has been around the pool so long they smell of chlorine
f. A sycophant, friendly but passive
g. Gets promoted by tyrants, and votes with tyrants as part of the deal
h. Sometimes gets the top job when the tyrant dies/leaves
i. Gets promoted on convenient soundbites and how clean their pool is

6. The Classic Apparatchik
a. Commonly found outside true capitalism i.e. government/local council/utility company etc.
b. Greasy pole climber, slowly does it
c. Garners an amazing/unbelievable pension
d. Is a serial sunflower
e. Never takes a risk
f. Is a technically-opinionated expert who gets shifted into management
g. Will move around the organisation as suits the directors, is malleable
h. Goes on all the management junkets for silly new things
i. Spends days flitting around, does not focus

7. The Glass Ceiling Victim
a. Talented technically and also has good interpersonal skills
b. Is a solid and reliable hard worker
c. Is high-performing, and high in integrity
d. Well-liked by their team/peers/some of their leaders
e. Hardworking but is naïve about, or unwilling to play, politics
f. Other less effective people get promoted ahead of them in the queue
g. They perhaps lack the confidence to back themselves
h. Some are simply unable to face the thought of the pressure of high office

Of course, there are some great leaders out there. Chapter 16 contains a list of the competencies you might find in the strong and caring leader. This is the person who leads the organisation that writes an adaptive strategy, and delivers on this strategy, time and time again. This is that 1% special person at the top of that 20% 'best leaders' group.

16.0 The Strong And Caring Leader

I am sure we can all write a list of qualities we believe would be exhibited by our ideal leader. My list looks like this:

Someone strong who:
- Sets clear expectations and goals
- Is an efficient and concise communicator
- Won't let stupid comments/actions slide by unnoticed
- Handles feedback in an adult and mature way
- Admits it when they're wrong and apologises
- Speaks truth to power
- Fails fast
- Removes barriers
- Delivers constructive feedback
- Relentlessly follows up
- Focuses on a handful of simple, strategic things
- Leads by influence 80% of the time, and direct instruction 20% of the time
- Knows when it's time to abandon this fight and move to a compromise

Someone caring who:
- Nurtures relationships
- Gives you feedback, elegantly
- Asks your advice
- Anticipates your needs
- Sets realistic goals
- Adjusts goals and expectations when appropriate
- Creates opportunities for growth and learning
- Encourages upward feedback and acts on it
- Reacts well to bad news
- Asks "What can I do to help you?"
- Makes you feel good about yourself

Of course, this is another set of subjective labels and aspirations. I would expect most people would aspire to these qualities. They are all closer to results than behaviours (which must be objective and observable).

If we were to pinpoint the behaviours that make up each of these labels, we could probably get closer to agreeing what would result in these qualities. By 'pinpointing' I mean spelling out the actual observable verbal and physical behaviours. For example, if someone 'reacts well to bad news', what would you see them do and hear them say? Perhaps the recipient listened without interrupting. Perhaps they did not speak until the whole story had been explained. Maybe they said something encouraging like, "Well that's bad news for sure but I am very pleased you told me. I would like to help you sort this out. What do you suggest happens next?"

In organisations, ambitious people can get high up in the hierarchy by having a good intellect, by being energetic, by being a good improviser or even just by dumb luck. Once you're there, you can select what kind of leader you want to be. The very best leaders I know have been in the mould typified by the maxim: "Train people well enough so they can leave, treat them well enough so they don't want to."

17.0 Epilogue

My friend, the late and great Professor Bill Abernathy used to answer a lot of my questions with the phrase "Yeah, I think some guys from Ohio State came up with that theory first." That was his stock answer when he couldn't remember which competing academic first had a key idea during the development phase of behavioural science. I remember trying to find out where the principle that antecedents have about a 20% effect on prompting behaviour came from, and sure enough, that was his answer. Pareto keeps popping up everywhere, and as previously mentioned it's an empirical law; it keeps appearing, scientists want to prove it (or disprove it) and they can't.

My endeavour in this book was to introduce behavioural science to the subject of strategy. There are many counter-intuitive norms in applying science to human relations. I suppose it's because you never get a truly controlled environment with humans (thankfully). The counter-intuitive element keeps popping up too; you want to shout at someone when it's actually the right time to comfort them.

Another friend from the world of behaviour, Dr Richard Kazbour said: "Behaviourally speaking, each time we change strategy we feel better, even if none of our previous fifteen strategies actually achieved any results. Negative reinforcement has a disastrous impact on our own ability to promote an accurate reality. Because we feel good in our strategizing by simply hoping for a better future, we're tricked into a state of behavioural dormancy."

I have attempted in this book to promote the truth, to promote the value of accurately measuring what's happening prior to commencing or changing, in fact, prior to embarking on any journey. Typically, all the classic workplace distractions seem to work against helping us keep something real and keep it simple. The forces of our better angels need to be protected and nurtured and this is achieved by staying strong, keeping things real, keeping them honest.

I like this quote by Aaron Sorkin: "The 'greater fool' is an economic term. It's a patsy. For the rest of us to profit, we need a greater fool, someone who will buy long and sell short. Most people spend their life trying not to be the greater fool; we toss them the hot potato, we dive for their seat when the music stops. The greater fool is someone with the perfect blend of self-delusion and ego to think that they can succeed where others have failed." Of course, plenty of great things have been achieved by these apparent quixotic fools, I guess that's what it feels like in the beginning of every great achievement. The 'greater fools' certainly serve up the most learning opportunities for themselves.

I wish you luck.
Howard Lees, Bollington, January 2019.

Appendix A - Examples of Adaptive Strategies

Strategies are both environmental and situational. Fictional strategy examples will never fully resonate with everyone. Nevertheless, to illustrate what could be included in an adaptive strategy, we have produced two here:

(Example 1) Adaptive Personal Strategic Plan

Name: Programme Director, Icabod Construction, running a water company's programme of works, value c. £400m/yr over 5 years.
Mission – Deliver the programme safely. Develop our people. Enhance our reputation.

Strategic plan

1. **What** is it that I want to achieve?
   - To deliver the programme of works on time and on budget.
   - Create an environment that encourages discretionary effort.
   - Develop a client relationship that facilitates success.
   - Win the next 5-year programme with this client.
2. **Why** do I want this goal?
   - It's a great opportunity for coaching our future superstars.
   - My career is predicated on success on this programme of work.
   - I must have something that keeps me learning, interested and active.
3. **Who** else is involved in the realisation of this goal?
   - Our contractor team.
   - The client team.
   - The supply chain and stakeholders for this programme.
   - Our wider business.
4. **When** is the result required?
   - Initially, by the end of this year.
   - Ultimately, after 5 years.
5. **Where** will this be happening?
- In the programme office and water company area.

How

- I am self-motivated and a good self-starter.
- I need to develop a great workplace environment for our people.
- I must keep the client in hand, protect my people from theirs.
- I utilise simple 'to-do' lists, collect my reinforcement by crossing things off.
- I will be strict when it comes to effective meetings and communications, and coach others to do the same.
- I must focus on coaching my direct reports and allowing them to do their jobs.
- I must only do my own job and coach my direct reports to do the same.
- Monitoring - I keep an eye on my set of simple indicators, tweak as necessary.

Test your stated results and behaviours with these additional questions:

1. What's your unique value proposition?
   - We have already won this programme in competition with the UK's best contractors.
   - This is the kind of work we have done well for the last 50 years, we have a great track record.
   - We are the only UK contractor with an accredited behavioural safety programme.
   - We have a mature team and a solid support network.
   - We are the only UK contractor with a behavioural programme for leadership.
2. How is what you could offer different to what's happening now?
   - It's not, this is our company's primary activity.
3. What would you be willing to give up in order to achieve your goals?
   - We are happy to 'do more for less' as long as our people get valuable experiences out of it.
   - Overall control on staff appointments, happy to second client people into our team.
4. What have you decided not to do?
   - Partner with other contractors.
   - Go out to market for prices, we will stay loyal to our supply chain.

- Anything that patronises our people, e.g. going to fancy London dinners in fancy clothes, collecting meaningless awards, employee of the month etc.
5. Which activities mentioned fit together and reinforce each other?
   - The management team will all maintain 'to-do' lists.
   - Meetings will be short, so we will have more time for thinking.
   - Email will be infrequent in comparison with face-to-face conversations or calls. We will mostly talk to each other.
   - I 'walk and coach' which is very effective at setting up an environment free from distractions.
   - I will coach the client to fit in with our stated cultural norms for meetings etc.
   - Monitoring – I keep an eye on all the usual indicators, tweak as necessary.
6. Where is the continual improvement in realising this strategy coming from?
   - Every day is a new learning opportunity, lots of creativity will be required.
   - Monthly climate surveys will generate high levels of feedback which I must ensure is acted upon in a timely manner.
   - We will focus on execution and deliver our projects, reporting will be simple.
   - I will ask for dissenting voices, and we will follow up on every point.
   - I will encourage the client to follow our lead.
   - Everyone's intellectual capacity will increase.

Barriers

Are there any obvious barriers to success?
- We need one or two more staff to help fill the inevitable gaps.
- The sell to the client is going to be hard, a strategy is required as well as help from our operational directors.
- Keeping our support service company directors off our people's back will be tough.
- The client's directors may resist the changes to their norms.

Next steps
- Write tactics for the above

(Example 2) Adaptive Personal Strategic Plan
Name: Managing Director, Icabod Removals, c £12m pa turnover, removals company in Crewe, Cheshire.
Mission – Deliver our customers' possessions on time and safely. Enhance our reputation.

Strategic plan
1. **What** is it that I want to achieve?
   - To maintain the quantity and quality of work for us and our workforce.
   - Maintain our environment for continued discretionary effort.
   - Maintain our sustainable turnover >£10m, <£15m per annum.
   - Maintain our staff numbers, train and mentor our new starts.
2. **Why** do I want this goal?
   - We like what we have now, the whole team would like to maintain it.
   - Our business model has worked for 25 years, it works well.
   - Our business is a prime candidate for selling, we will continue to resist.
   - The workers are fast owning the business, this is a sustainable model.
3. **Who** else is involved in the realisation of this goal?
   - Our removals teams, the office staff, our regular business customers.
   - The garage, maintenance team.
   - The bank, our accountants, our insurers, our partners.
4. **When** is the result required?
   - Initially, to maintain this year's targets.
   - Ongoing.
5. **Where** will this be happening?
   - Mostly Cheshire, although we also move people in and out of the county.

How
- I need to maintain a great workplace environment for our people.
- We must keep tabs on our pricing, keep good records of moves and feedback.
- I utilise my simple 'to-do' lists, and encourage others to do the same.
- We are strict on the details in contracts, communications etc.
- We must continue to train our next client managers.
- Monitor - I keep an eye on my set of simple indicators, tweak as necessary.

Do your stated results and behaviours withstand testing?
1. What's your unique value proposition?
   - We have been around a long time; our yard is in a prime position in Crewe.
   - We hire locals and EU nationals, we have a good balance.
   - We are the right size for our kind of work and our reach.
   - We have a great track record.
   - We support local events, we advertise at Alex.
   - Our fleet is modern, and our processes are solid.
2. How is what you could offer different to what's happening now?
   - It's not, this is our company's primary activity.
3. What would you be willing to give up in order to achieve your goals?
   - We may have to renew our fleet for electric vehicles at some point.
   - We may have to change our recruitment depending on Brexit.
   - I am keen to step down and hand over to a successor in the next 5 years.
4. What have you decided not to do?
   - Merge with our major competitor.
   - Buy our major competitor.
   - Borrow money and enlarge our company.
   - Cut our prices to suit the periodic out of town chancers.
5. Which activities mentioned fit together and reinforce each other?
   - I 'walk and coach' the staff, which is very effective.
   - Our staff and workforce should continue to buy shares into the company, their dividends link them directly to efficiency.
   - Everyone has a real job here, we will not hire any pointless fancy titles.
   - I will keep an eye on all my usual indicators, tweak as necessary.
   - Perspective - We are not overly driven by todays financials.
6. Where is the continual improvement in realising this strategy coming from?
   - Every day is a new opportunity to help folks get better.
   - I need to identify a succession plan and get that going.
   - We have an excellent reputation, lots of genuine plaudits, this strategy will continue to support that.
   - We will continue to encourage feedback, we will follow up on every point.
   - We will encourage our clients to be candid with their feedback.

Barriers

Are there any obvious barriers to success?

- Uncertainty - Brexit is creating uncertainty for our EU nationals.
- We had some defaulting clients this year, this may get worse.
- We may have to think more about taking payment/deposits prior to work.
- Moving to electric vehicles needs a good plan; investment vs lower maintenance/fuel cost.
- I need to get a successor in place while I am still alive.
- Insurance costs are rising much higher than reasonable.
- We may not be able to hold on to our prime spot in town much longer (new road plans).

Next steps

- Write tactics for the above

Appendix B - Behavioural Science Terms Used in This Booklet

Behavioural science is the science of human behaviour; it is founded on using data and analysis to come to conclusions about what is happening in the interactions of people. Objectivity is at the core of behavioural science. Behavioural Management Techniques (BMT) is a blend of behavioural science tools and project management skills.

I have written a booklet called *Notes on Behavioural Management Techniques* which discusses behavioural terms and offers more explanation than is covered here. This chapter should be enough to help you with the terms I mention in this booklet.

Psychologists seek to understand what is going on inside the mind, to modify these internal phenomena and in doing so achieve behaviour change. Behavioural scientists observe the behaviour, seek to modify the external environment - which is the only thing we really have influence over anyway - and in doing so, achieve behaviour change. Behavioural science sees each person as an individual who desires a totally unique set of reinforcers from their environment (their world).

Both mainstream psychology and behavioural science are used in seeking to change behaviour. Critically, behavioural science has a greater verifiable record of achieving this and is also far easier for people to learn and apply.

A number of scientific terms are used in this booklet. These are described here:

Antecedents

An antecedent is a request or prompt; something which is attempting to drive a particular behaviour. A sign that says, 'don't smoke', a speed sign, and a plan detailing how you will deliver a project are all antecedents. Antecedents are quite poor at driving behaviour if they are not paired with consequences. We are all regularly bombarded with antecedents.

Some antecedents are very good at demanding our attention. I care about the weather forecast the day before I'm going on a long walk. I care about the flight information board when I'm flying somewhere. I check what day I have to put the bins out. I look at the fuel gauge in my car when driving. Unfortunately, many work-based antecedents do not have the desired effect. Procedures, safety rules, notice boards, minutes of meetings and requests by email will all work in part, but will only work well if paired with consequences.

Behaviour
Behaviours are 'what we say and do'. They are entirely objective and measurable. It is common to see lists of behaviours in organisations that include 'communicating' or 'trust'. These are not true behaviours, as they are subjective. In contrast, 'saying "hello" to the receptionist' is a behaviour. Behaviours should fulfil the pinpointing rules (see below).

BMT - Behavioural Management Techniques
Behavioural Management Techniques (BMT) is a unique blend of applied behavioural science tools and project management skills. The aim of BMT is to get people to do the right things because they want to, not because they have to.

Consequences
The impact of consequences is the primary influencer of our behaviour. What happens to us following our behaviour will affect the likelihood of us performing the same behaviour again under similar circumstances.

Behavioural science states that there are two main consequence types that result in a behaviour occurring/recurring or stopping. They are defined as Reinforcement and Punishment. These fundamental principles are as follows:
1. If behaviour is maintained or increases, it has been subject to reinforcement.
2. If behaviour reduces or stops it has been subjected to punishment.

The consequence in each individual case is defined by its impact on behaviour. More detail can be found in the Hollin booklet *Notes on Behavioural Management Techniques*.

Extinction
Extinction is the process of being ignored. It can be very painful if you are the recipient of it. It is also a useful tool to use if you wish someone's irritating behaviour to go away. A subset of extinction is the extinction burst, an emotional outburst of some kind (usually verbal). This usually occurs when the behaviour is receding and is a good indicator that it is.

Environment
The environment is the immediate location of a person, be it in their office, living room, their car; wherever the behaviour is occurring. A person's behaviour is mostly driven by the consequences that have followed the behaviour (or similar behaviours) in the past. The environment will dictate the consequences you experience and this includes the other people in the room, office etc. Small changes in environment can result in significant changes in the behaviour of an individual. The environment affects us and we affect the environment.

For example, imagine an office full of people. Take one person out of the office and replace them with a different person and the environment has changed. The change could be very significant depending on who left and who came in.

Pinpointing
Pinpointing is the process used to make sure that a behaviour is described accurately. Something is pinpointed when it complies with all the following rules:
1. It can be seen or heard.
2. It can be measured or counted.
3. Two people would always agree that the same behaviour occurred or not.
4. It is active (something is occurring).

People who learn pinpointing can quickly develop skills which reduce the amount of assumption in their environment. This reduction of (sometimes destructive) assumptions increases the amount of informed comment, decision and discussion.

It is advisable to gather data on situations via observations and keep notes of who actually said/did what. This significantly reduces the chance of unnecessary conflict created by assumption.

Pinpointing is a very useful skill for business. Next time someone relates something to you, if you are unsure of the message you can say, "Can you pinpoint that for me please?"

Shaping

Shaping is a simple concept which is very difficult to master. It recognises that you can't get from step one to step ten in one vertical stride. You sometimes have to first write out steps two through nine and then carry them all out, one step at a time.

People sometimes tell me, "I want to say this to my boss." Before you say anything you need to predict the chances of it being received the right way by your boss. "Not very good," will often be the reply. Unfortunately, you have to shape to the goal you want to achieve, and this usually means a time-consuming set of steps which will shape the environment so that you can eventually say what you want to say and it will have the desired effect.

Shaping is not for the impatient, and a realisation that patience is the key can take time for some people. Sometimes, there is no other choice. You can't force the situation to move any faster so your options are slow shaping or nothing. Many very reinforcing tools we use these days do not help us forge a patient approach, e.g. email and voicemail. It is not naturally reinforcing taking the extra time to consider, "Is this the right thing to say? Does something else have to be achieved before I can say this and get what I want?"

Shaping is inherent in everything we learn. If you want to play an instrument, you repeat and adapt until you can play the tune. Anything that requires mastery requires repetition, reflection and adaptation. Putting a group of employees to work effectively and safely requires a leader to choose carefully who will work with whom. It requires trial and error to find the best combinations. Iteration is trying things out and seeing what the result is, adjusting and trying again - this is shaping, it works, it's the only thing that does work when building a team. This is how you succeed at getting all the right people on the bus, sat in the right seats.

Appendix C -
Further Recommended Reading

I like to read. In fact, I am the guy on the train reading a book while most of the other travellers are frantically trying to get their internet connection restored. These books are all packed with varied wisdom of some kind. There are a number of useful shorter publications you could download from our website (www.hollin.co.uk) should you wish to start with an entrée.

1.   What Got You Here Won't Get You There - Marshall Goldsmith
2.   The Strategy Book – Max McKeown
3.   The 80/20 Principle – Richard Koch
4.   Turn the Ship Around! - L David Marquet
5.   Maverick - Ricardo Semler
6.   Why Employees Don't Do What They're Supposed To Do - Ferdinand F. Fournies
7.   Bringing Out the Best in People - Aubrey Daniels
8.   The Hungry Spirit - Charles Handy
9.   Coaching for Improved Work Performance - Ferdinand F. Fournies
10. Performance Management - Aubrey Daniels and James E. Daniels
11. The Sin of Wages - William Abernathy
12. Other People's Habits - Aubrey C Daniels
13. The Tipping Point - Malcolm Gladwell
14. Myself and Other More Important Matters - Charles Handy
15. Open Minds - Andy Law
16. Leading Change - John P Kotter
17. The Empowered Manager - Peter Block
18. The 20% Solution - John Cotter
19. Measure of a Leader - Aubrey C. Daniels and James E. Daniels

20. The Elephant and the Flea - Charles Handy
21. How the Mighty Fall - Jim Collins
22. Good to Great - Jim Collins
23. Body Language - Allan Pease
24. Experiment at Work - Andy Law
25. OBM Applied - Manuel Rodriguez, Daniel Sundberg, and Shannon Biagi
26. The Empty Raincoat - Charles Handy
27. Unlock Behaviors, Unleash Profits - Leslie Braksick
28. Built to Last - Jim Collins and Jerry I. Porras
29. On Writing - Steven King
30. Don't Shoot the Dog - Karen Prior
31. Learning Reinforcement Theory - Fred S. Keller
32. The Seven-Day Weekend - Ricardo Semler
33. The First 90 Days - Michael Watkins
34. How to Deal with Difficult People - Ursula Markham
35. The Leadership Pipeline - Ram Charan, Stephen Drotter and James Noel
36. Understanding Organisations - Charles Handy
37. The Principles of Scientific Management - F.W. Taylor

Appendix D -
Other Hollin Publications

All Hollin Publications are available at http://www.hollin.co.uk/shop

POWER COACHING
By Howard Lees
ISBN number 978-0-9575211-2-4

THE TOO BUSY TRAP
By Howard Lees
ISBN number 987-0-9575211-1-7

THE STEPS BEFORE STEP ONE
By Howard Lees
ISBN number 978-0-9563114-9-8

NOTES ON BEHAVIOURAL MANAGEMENT TECHNIQUES
By Howard Lees
ISBN number 978-0-9563114-1-2

IDEAS FOR WIMPS
By Howard Lees
ISBN number 978-0-9563114-6-7

HOW TO EMPTY THE TOO HARD BOX
By Howard Lees
ISBN number 978-0-9563114-4-3

HOW TO ESCAPE FROM CLOUD CUCKOO LAND
By Howard Lees
ISBN number 978-0-9563114-8-1

SAFETY LEADERSHIP
By Howard Lees
ISBN number 978-0-9575211-4-8

BMT SCORECARDS
By Howard Lees
ISBN number 978-0-9575211-1-7

BEHAVIOURAL COACHING
By Howard Lees
ISBN number 978-0-9563114-2-9

notes: